UNDERSTANDING WEATHER PATTERNS

by Nancy Dickmann

PEBBLE
a capstone imprint

Pebble is published by Capstone,
1710 Roe Crest Drive, North Mankato, Minnesota 56003
www.capstonepub.com

Library of Congress Cataloging-in-Publication data is available on the Library of Congress website.
ISBN: 978-1-9771-3350-2 (library binding)
ISBN: 978-1-9771-3344-1 (paperback)
ISBN: 978-1-9771-5520-7 (eBook PDF)

Summary: Describes weather patterns, such as seasons and wind and rain patterns, including what causes weather patterns.

Editorial Credits
Editor: Mandy Robbins; Designer: Dina Her; Media Researcher: Tracy Cummins; Production Specialist: Katy LaVigne

Photo Credits
iStockphoto: Marilyn Nieves, 27, Photo_Concepts, 5; Science Source: Spencer Sutton, 17, VICTOR DE SCHWANBERG, cover, design element, 1; Shutterstock: Africa Studio, 9, Alan Budman, 19, Chayantorn Tongmorn, 15, Color4260, design element, Denis Blofield, 20, Designua, 11, Dmitry Polonskiy, 21, Earl D. Walker, 26, elRoce, 28–29, Johannes Zielcke, 10, LazarenkoD, 24, Makhnach_S, design element, Mike Focus, 7, Nasky, 12, neenawat khenyothaa, 23 bottom, Patrick Foto, 4, Rod Zadeh, 18, S.Borisov, 8, serkan senturk, 23 top, VectorMine, 25, Vixit, 13

Printed and bound in the USA. PO3837

TABLE OF CONTENTS

Words in **bold** are in the glossary.

WHAT IS WEATHER?

What is it like outside right now? How warm is it? Is it sunny or cloudy? Is it raining or snowing? Can you feel a breeze? You are describing the weather. The **conditions** in the air around us make up weather.

Weather is different in different places. Even in one place, it often changes. It can change from one hour to the next. It can change from day to day. It can go from being warm and sunny to cool and rainy. Weather also changes from season to season.

Regular Patterns

Sometimes the weather stays the same. It may stay hot and sunny for weeks. This is a weather pattern. It may be rainy at the same time each year. This is a pattern too.

Every place has its own weather patterns. They often repeat each year. In some places, there are fewer patterns. The weather changes are harder to **predict**. Predicting the weather is called **forecasting**.

A weather reporter gives the forecast on TV.

Forecasters look at many things. One is **air pressure**. Falling air pressure means rain or storms are likely.

AIR PRESSURE

Did you know that air has weight? It is made of tiny **particles**. Lots of them together are very heavy. Their weight pushes down on Earth's surface. This is called air pressure.

SEASONS

Seasons are a weather pattern. Many places have four seasons in a year. Other places have just one or two. Each season has its own weather. The seasons repeat each year.

summer

fall

In places with four seasons, summer days are long. It is warm and often sunny. In fall, it gets cooler. Winter is cold and sometimes snowy. The days are short, and nights are long. In spring, it gets warmer. It rains often.

winter

spring

What Causes Seasons?

Earth spins on its **axis**. But Earth is not straight up and down. It is tilted. This spinning causes days and nights. Earth also travels around the sun. Sometimes, the top half points toward the sun. Sometimes it points away.

The sun appears lower in the sky when it is winter.

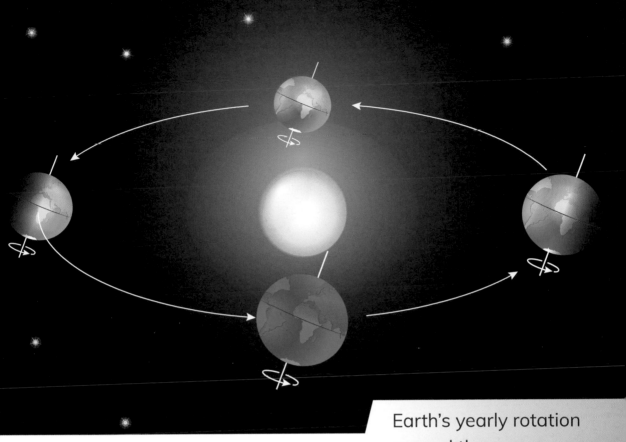

Earth's yearly rotation around the sun

When Earth's top half points toward the sun, it gets more light. It gets more heat too. The days are longer. It is summer there. The bottom half points away from the sun. There is less light and heat. It is winter there.

night

equator

day

Sun

Earth

Tropical Seasons

An invisible line goes around the middle of Earth. This line is called the **equator**. The areas near it are called the **tropics**.

The air in the tropics is warm. Water **vapor** there rises to form clouds. When warm air cools down, it can't hold the water anymore. The water falls as rain.

Seasons are different in the tropics. It stays warm all year. It rains a lot too. There may be a dry season and a rainy season.

WIND

The sun heats Earth. Some places get more heat than others. Winds help even out the heat. Big differences in temperature make strong winds. Winds also even out air pressure.

WHAT CAUSES WIND?

When air warms up, it rises. Cool air rushes in to replace it. We feel this as wind. As air rises, it gets cooler. It moves toward Earth's **poles**. There, it gets cold again. The air sinks back down.

Wind blows from an area of high pressure. It blows toward an area of low pressure. Winds have patterns. They often blow in the same direction. Different parts of Earth have different wind patterns.

Jet Streams

Jet streams are narrow bands of wind. They blow high above Earth's surface. A jet stream blows from west to east. Its winds are very strong. They are strongest in winter.

Jet streams don't always blow in the same place. Sometimes the jet stream moves a bit north. Sometimes it moves south. It pushes large areas of air with it. It moves weather systems.

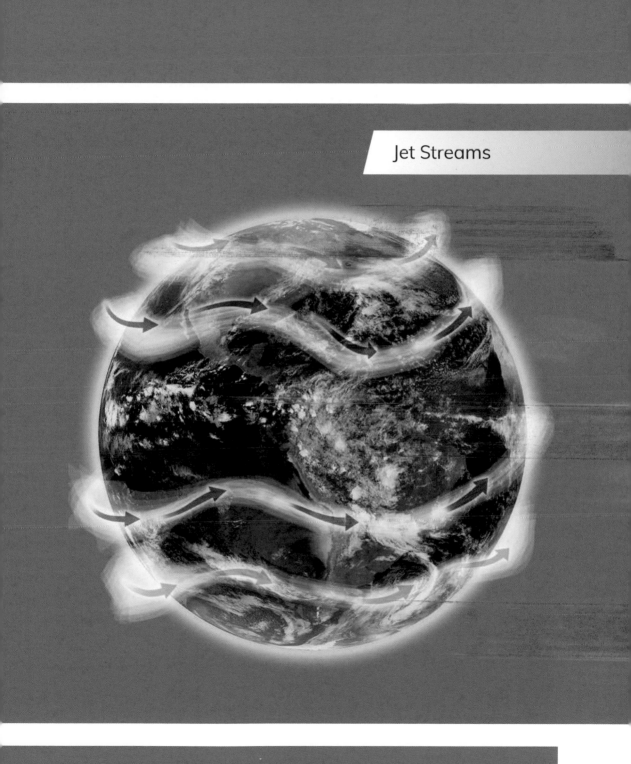

The Polar Vortex

The most northern and most southern parts of Earth are the North and South Poles. It is very cold at Earth's poles. The air pressure is low. Strong winds swirl around the poles. They keep cold air trapped there. This is called a polar vortex. There is one at each pole.

Sometimes the polar vortex expands. It spreads very cold weather. It can even break up. Areas of cold air travel far from the poles.

OCEANS AND WEATHER

Water is really good at taking in heat. The oceans take in heat from the air. The warm air heats the top layer of water. Near Earth's poles, there is less heat from the sun. Water there is cooler.

Near the equator, water warms the land.

Water moves throughout the oceans. Colder water sinks, just as cold air does. Then warm water rushes in to replace it. This movement causes **currents**. Currents move warm water from the tropics to the poles. Currents help warm some land masses. They cool land in other areas.

El Niño

In the tropics, currents move from east to west. So do winds. When warm currents hit a large area of land, warm water builds up. A weather pattern called El Niño helps send the warm water back out to sea.

An El Niño happens every few years. Warm water starts to flow back east. This makes winds slow down. The winds might change direction. These changes cause heavy rain in some places. They cause **droughts** in others.

RAIN PATTERNS

Moving Over Mountains

Moving air sometimes reaches mountains. It has to rise to pass over them. As the air rises, it cools. In cool air, clouds can't hold as much water. On one side of the mountains, the water falls as rain or snow.

Once the air passes over the mountains, it has little water left. On this side, rain rarely falls. This area is called a rain shadow. **Deserts** are often found in rain shadows.

rain shadow

Drought and Heat Waves

Sometimes it rains less than usual over a period of time. This is called a drought. Changes in the jet stream can cause droughts. During a drought, plants and animals may not get enough water.

Sometimes the weather is hotter than normal. This is a heat wave. It might last for weeks. Changes in the jet stream can cause heat waves too.

Hurricane Season

A hurricane is a strong storm. It brings heavy rain. Hurricanes form over the ocean. Their wind spins around in a circle. Hurricanes can move over land. They bring strong winds.

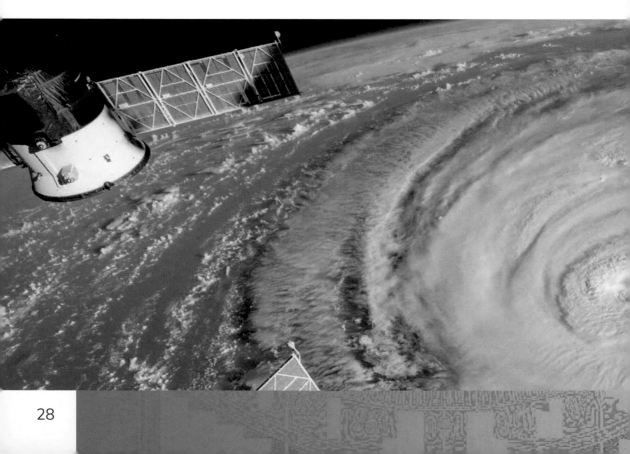

Hurricanes often happen in the same season each year. Hurricane season is just one type of weather pattern. There are many others. Looking at patterns helps us predict the weather.

GLOSSARY

air pressure (AYR PRESH-uhr)—the weight of air pushing against something

axis (AK-siss)—a straight line around which an object rotates

condition (kuhn-DI-shuhn)—the general state of something

current (KUHR-uhnt)—the movement of water in a river or an ocean

desert (DE-zuhrt)—a dry area with little rain

drought (DROUT)—a long period of weather with little or no rainfall

equator (i-KWAY-tuhr)—an imaginary line around the middle of Earth

forecast (FOR-kast)—to predict future changes in the weather

particle (PAR-tuh-kuhl)—a very tiny piece of something

pole (POHL)—the most northern and most southern parts of Earth

predict (pri-DIKT)—to say what you think will happen in the future

tropics (TRAH-piks)—a warm region of Earth that is near the equator

vapor (VAY-pur)—a gas made from liquid

READ MORE

Gibbons, Gail. *The Reasons for Seasons*. New York: Holiday House, 2019.

Rajczak, Michael. *Deadly Droughts*. New York: Gareth Stevens Publishing, 2016.

Stewart, Melissa. *Hurricane Watch*. New York: HarperCollins, 2015.

INTERNET SITES

Climate Kids
climatekids.nasa.gov/ocean/

National Weather Service Education
weather.gov/owlie/

Weather
dkfindout.com/uk/earth/weather/

INDEX